Career Expert Files

What Plumbers Need to Know

Diane Lindsey Reeves

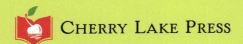

Published in the United States of America by Cherry Lake Publishing Group
Ann Arbor, Michigan
www.cherrylakepublishing.com

Reading Adviser: Beth Walker Gambro, MS, Ed., Reading Consultant, Yorkville, IL

Photo Credits: © AYO Production/Shutterstock, cover; © Monkey Business Images/Shutterstock, 5; © Monkey Business Images/Shutterstock, 7; © Leo_nik/Shutterstock, 8; © Elena Shashkina/Shutterstock, 9; © Oleg Opryshko/Shutterstock, 11; © CandyRetriever/Shutterstock, 12; © Pavel L Photo and Video/Shutterstock, 13; © Africa Studio/Shutterstock, 14; © Towfiqu ahamed barbhuiya/Shutterstock, 15; © AYO Production/Shutterstock, 17; © Bilanol/Shutterstock, 18; © JRJFin/Shutterstock, 19; © Aleksandr Finch/Shutterstock, 21; © Andrew Angelov/Shutterstock, 22; © kaninw/Shutterstock, 23; © RosnaniMusa/Shutterstock, 24; © pixelheadphoto digitalskillet/Shutterstock, 25; © Microgen/Shutterstock, 27; © Yau Ming Low/Shutterstock, 28; © Kirkam/Shutterstock, 29; © NT_Studio/Shutterstock, 31

Copyright © 2026 by Cherry Lake Publishing Group
All rights reserved. No part of this book may be reproduced or utilized in any form or by any means without written permission from the publisher.

Cherry Lake Press is an imprint of Cherry Lake Publishing Group.

Library of Congress Cataloging-in-Publication Data has been filed and is available at catalog.loc.gov.

Cherry Lake Publishing Group would like to acknowledge the work of the Partnership for 21st Century Learning, a Network of Battelle for Kids. Please visit Battelle for Kids online for more information.

Printed in the United States of America

Note from publisher: Websites change regularly, and their future contents are outside of our control. Supervise children when conducting any recommended online searches for extended learning opportunities.

Diane Lindsey Reeves likes to write books that help students figure out what they want to be when they grow up. She mostly lives in Washington, D.C., but spends as much time as she can in North Carolina and South Carolina with her grandkids.

CONTENTS

Introduction:
In the Know | 4

Chapter 1:
Plumbers Know...How to Go With the Flow | 6

Chapter 2:
Plumbers Know...All About Plumbing | 10

Chapter 3:
Plumbers Know...The Tools of the Trade | 16

Chapter 4:
Plumbers Know...How to Work Safely | 20

Chapter 5:
**Plumbers Know...How to Find
the Job They Want | 26**

Stop, Think, and Write | 30
Things to Do If You Want to Be a Plumber | 30
Learn More | 31
Glossary, Index | 32

In the Know

Every career you can imagine has one thing in common: It takes an expert. Career experts need to know more about how to do a specific job than other people do. That's how everyone from plumbers to rocket scientists gets their job done.

Sometimes it takes years of college study to learn what they need to know. Other times, people learn by working alongside someone who is already a career expert. No matter how they learn, it takes a career expert to do any job well.

Take plumbers, for instance. Most people don't give plumbing a thought until something goes wrong. Most days, the plumbing systems in homes and businesses work like a charm.

It's those rare days that this doesn't happen that make plumbers so popular. Plumbers come through with knowledge and skill to solve problems that most people can't even begin to solve themselves.

Plumbers are good at:

- Using algebra and geometry to lay out plumbing plans
- Working with different tools
- Reading **blueprints**
- Solving plumbing problems

CHAPTER 1

Plumbers Know... How to Go With the Flow

Plumbers work on two main types of plumbing problems. They design and install new plumbing systems for homes and businesses. They also repair existing plumbing problems.

Plumbing systems carry water to faucets and appliances. They also remove waste. A plumber's job is to install pipes that bring water into a building and carry it out. They also make repairs when systems break down with leaks or clogs.

Another part of a plumber's job is to install the fixtures that use water. This includes water heaters, toilets, sinks, and appliances. It is important that these fixtures are installed by someone who knows what they are doing. Leaks can cause big problems!

Old or clogged pipes can cause leaks. You can wrap the leak with tape or put a bucket under it before calling a plumber!

Each city has its own sewer system that runs beneath our feet. We rely on plumbers to keep these systems running.

Plumbing systems are connected to huge networks of sewers that take **wastewater** to water treatment plants. Most sewer systems are underground. Some plumbers clean, repair, and replace sewer lines.

Putting in new sewer lines is complicated. It involves important calculations that determine how well the sewer will work. Plumbers work with other tradespeople to get the job done.

There is a lot to learn about being a plumber. Most plumbers are trained through a 4-year **apprenticeship**. Apprenticeships include some classroom learning and lots of paid on-the-job training. In many U.S. states, plumbers must get a license. A license allows plumbers to run their own businesses and get insurance. A license is needed to obtain building permits and pass inspections.

Plumbing is a high-demand trade career. It pays well and offers opportunities to be your own boss. Many plumbers end up running their own plumbing companies. People consider themselves lucky when they find a good plumber!

SCRUB-A-DUB-DUB...

Before indoor plumbing, bath time was complicated. Someone had to bring in buckets of water from a well. They had to heat the water over a fireplace or stove. Then they poured it into a tub. These steps were repeated until the tub was full. It wasn't unusual for families to take turns bathing using the same bathwater. Pity the family member who had to go last! Since it was so difficult, people tended to bathe just once a week or less.

CHAPTER 2

Plumbers Know... All About Plumbing

On the surface, plumbing seems simple enough. You turn on a faucet and water comes out. You flush the toilet and waste goes away. Our plumbing systems work so well that we don't give them much thought. Plumbers put their knowledge and skills to work making that happen.

Plumbers know how water moves through underground pipes to get where it is needed. They make plans for how to move it throughout a house or business. They also know how drainage systems carry out wastewater. They make choices about the best drains, venting systems, and pipes to use for each job.

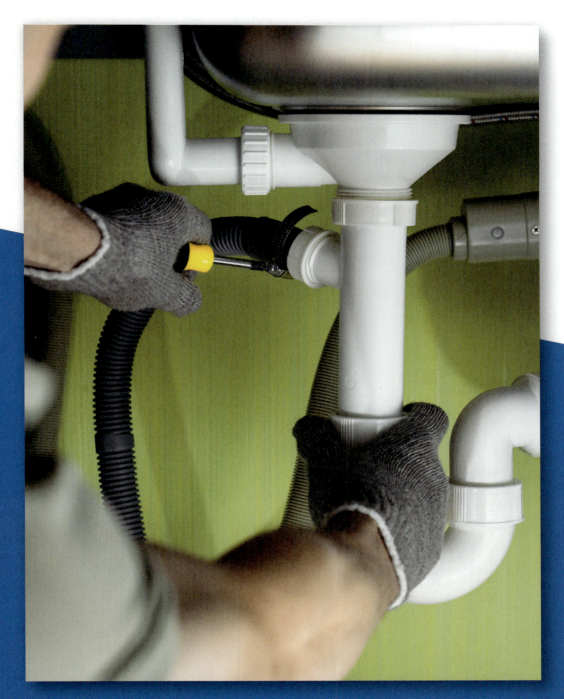

Each pipe in your house requires special attention. Even a small error can cause a big problem!

Cities make rules that plumbers have to follow. Rules may tell which size pipes to use, places where appliances can go, and how to connect plumbing to the city's sewer system.

Plumbers must follow local building rules. This includes getting the proper permits. City officials inspect their work to make sure it meets building codes.

Water is moved through structures in pipes. Cutting, fitting, and joining pipes are part of the job. Sometimes plumbers **solder** or **crimp** the pipes into place. Other times, they **thread** or glue them. This seems like a small detail. But knowing which technique to use in each situation is an important skill.

Crimping a pipe means using special tools to create a watertight seal. Plumbers are taught to do this.

Installing a toilet is no simple job. Even for experienced plumbers, the process can take up to 4 hours.

Plumbers also install plumbing fixtures like sinks, faucets, and toilets. All it takes is one loose seal to cause major problems. This is a job best left to the experts!

Troubleshooting is a skill that plumbers use on every job. That means they pinpoint problems and plan solutions. Many times, they are responding to emergency situations.

It could be a burst pipe, a backed-up sewer, or a broken water heater. Whatever the problem, quick answers and action are needed.

There's a lot to know about in plumbing. Customers rely on their plumbers to bring know-how and skills to the job.

WIPE-OUT!

Toilet paper wasn't available to buy until the 1850s. Before that, people had to clean themselves with whatever was handy. Options included rocks, leaves, grass, moss, animal fur, corncobs, coconut husks, sticks, sand, and seashells. Some people used pages from newspapers or magazines. Most people agree that toilet paper was a wonderful invention! Too much can clog pipes, though. That's where plumbers come in.

CHAPTER 3

Plumbers Know...
The Tools of the Trade

How do plumbers avoid getting into hot water? They use the right tools. Sure, you'll find some of these tools in any skilled tradesperson's toolbox. These include hammers, wrenches, screwdrivers, and the like. Doing plumbing right requires the right tools.

Plumbers work with a lot of pipes. The pipes are often made from a special plastic. These durable pipes can last for 100 years or more. They are lightweight and good for transporting liquids.

Plumbers must cut the long pieces of plastic pipe to fit specific places. They use pipe cutters with sharp cutting wheels or blades that rotate around a pipe to get clean, accurate cuts. They fit different sizes and shapes of pipe together with fittings called nuts and bolts. Adjustable pipe wrenches help them fasten pipes securely.

Inside a plumber's tool kit, you may find pliers, pipe wrenches, pipe benders, and more.

The last thing plumbers want to see is a leaky pipe. They seal the places where pipes fit together using special kinds of tape, putty, or sealants. Sometimes they need to **weld** pipes together. When using copper or other metal pipes, they may need to use a soldering torch. The process is a little easier when using plastic pipes. They can use chemicals called **solvent cement** to hold those together.

WHERE DOES WASTEWATER GO?

Wastewater flushed from toilets or drained from sinks goes out of your home into a sewer system. Sewers are large underground pipes that carry wastewater and human waste away from your home and neighborhood to wastewater treatment plants.

Wastewater treatment plants are usually located near a river or stream. Once the water has been safely cleaned, it is returned to the ecosystem. You'll be happy to know that drinking water and wastewater are treated separately.

Clogged pipes are a common plumbing problem. Smaller clogs can be fixed using a drain **auger** known as a plumber's snake. These small tools rotate slowly to push through stubborn clogs. For really tough clogs, they bring on a hydro jet. This tool uses pressured water to break down drain buildup and give pipes a good cleaning.

Plumbers use digital pipe cameras to look deep into a system's pipes. This lets them identify leaks and other problems. These tiny cameras are attached to hoses. Plumbers snake the hoses into a pipe to get a peek. Images are seen on small screens similar in size to a smartphone screen. Some hoses reach as far as 500 feet (152.4 meters). This helps plumbers look for problems from the pipe to the sewer line.

CHAPTER 4

Plumbers Know... How to Work Safely

Plumbers must dress for success. This starts with personal protection equipment (PPE). It includes gear you need to stay safe from head to toe.

Plumbing involves lots of cutting and sawing. Cut-resistant plumbing gloves can keep you safe from serious injury on the job. Rubber-soled, steel-toed shoes or boots are the best bet for footwear. Plumbers also use disposable shoe covers to keep their work environment and people's homes clean.

Plastic eyeglasses or goggles protect the eyes. Earplugs or muffs are used to protect ears from the noise of certain equipment. Jumpsuits or overalls protect clothes.

Protective goggles stop any liquids, chemicals, or dust from hurting the plumber's eyes.

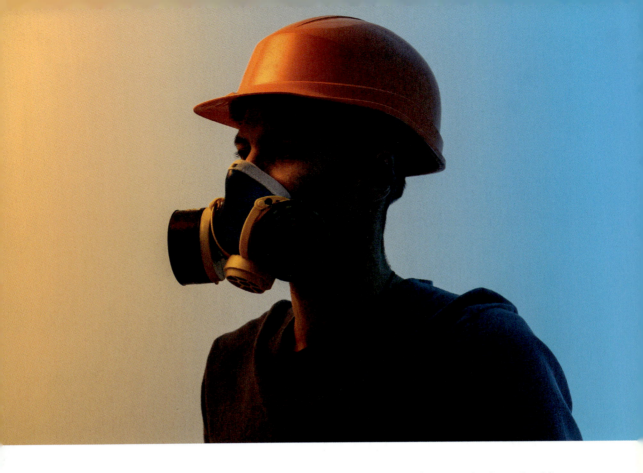

Respirators filter dangerous particles from the air before they can be breathed in. Some respirators also provide clean air from an outside source.

Wearing a face mask or **respirator** protects a plumber's lungs. Otherwise, pesky substances like mold spores, sewer gases, and dust can cause problems.

There are also smart ways plumbers stay safe on the job. Caution comes first. They must use it when working with equipment that gets hot. This includes hot water pipes.

They use caution when handling chemicals like toxic drain cleaners. They also use caution when working with electrical tools. All plumbers know that water and electricity do not mix!

Plumbers prevent injury by using good lifting techniques when working with heavy equipment. They can also prevent injuries by keeping work areas clean and organized. Plumbing involves hard physical labor. It is important to take breaks and stay hydrated.

GREEN PLUMBING

Many plumbers do their part to help customers conserve water and energy. They install low-flow toilets and showerheads to reduce the amount of water used for showering and flushing. Modern fixtures like tankless water heaters help save energy. These types of steps save customers money on water and energy bills. They also help protect the planet.

Plumbers often work outside in muddy, dusty conditions. They might leave work very dirty.

You can keep your hands clean, just like plumbers. Make sure to scrub for at least 20 seconds!

If ever there was a job where handwashing was necessary, plumbing is it. Plumbers come into contact with lots of germy surfaces and substances. Keeping hands clean protects plumbers from diseases and infections.

Probably the most important safety rule is to be prepared. Having the right tools is key for a plumber. Knowing who to call in an emergency is also key. The right resources make plumbers ready to tackle anything.

CHAPTER 5

Plumbers Know... How to Find the Job They Want

There are plenty of opportunities for plumbers to keep water flowing in new and old buildings. They may focus on homes or businesses. In many cases, plumbers take on whatever type of plumbing problem comes their way.

Some plumbers prefer to work on projects that keep them out of bathrooms and kitchens. They put in irrigation systems for homes, farms, or parks. These systems water yards, gardens, and crops and keep them growing.

Installing fire sprinkler systems is another way to use plumbing skills. These systems are installed in all kinds of structures. They are designed to release water when smoke or fire is detected. This is lifesaving work. People who install these systems are called sprinkler fitters.

Many buildings contain fire sprinkler systems. If it is a large office building or school, these systems may have taken weeks to install!

A number of other careers require similar training and problem-solving skills. Boilermakers are one example. Boilermakers are tradespeople who manufacture, install, and maintain **boilers**. Are you wondering what a boiler is? It is a large, closed container that heats water or other liquids. It generates electricity in buildings, factories, or ships.

Pipefitters and steamfitters install pipes and maintain piping systems used for chemicals, acids, or gases. These skilled craftspeople are called fitters. They work on commercial and industrial construction projects. Fitters must know how to handle hazardous materials safely.

HELP WANTED

The U.S. Department of Labor predicts that there will be 43,000 job openings for plumbers every year for the next decade. That's a lot of plumbers! Much of the demand comes from new construction projects. There will also be a need to replace plumbers who retire or move to other professions.

Stores like The Home Depot have all kinds of plumbing supplies, such as pipes and faucets.

Heating, ventilation, and air-conditioning (HVAC) installation technicians set up systems that heat and cool buildings. These systems require water and gas hookups. Plumbing skills also come in handy when jobs require installing **ductwork** throughout the building.

Next time you visit a large hardware store like The Home Depot or Lowe's, take a stroll in the plumbing section. You'll find all kinds of gadgets and gizmos needed in plumbing systems. Many people find careers manufacturing and selling this equipment.

Activity

Stop, Think, and Write

Can you imagine a world without plumbers? How do they make the places we live, work, and play better?

Get a separate sheet of paper. On one side, answer this question:

- *How do plumbers make the world a better place?*

On the other side of the paper:

- *Draw a picture or diagram showing how water gets to your house.*

Things to Do If You Want to Be a Plumber

Interested in plumbing? You don't have to wait until you're an adult to start preparing for this career. Here are some things you can do if you want to be a plumber someday:

NOW

- Figure out where water goes when you flush the toilet.
- Look under the sinks in your house to see the pipes that carry water in and out.
- With an adult, visit a construction site to see how plumbing systems are installed.
- Look into ways your family can conserve water and take good care of your home's plumbing system.

LATER

- Look into apprenticeship opportunities for plumbers.
- Consider what kind of plumbing you most want to do.
- Obtain a plumbing license and get to work.

Learn More

Books

Bethea, Nikole Brooks. *Toilets.* Minneapolis, MN: Jump! Inc., 2021.

Falconer, Sam. *Water Cycles: The Source of Life from Start to Finish.* New York, NY: DK Publishing, 2021.

Mara, Wil. *Be a Plumber.* Ann Arbor, MI: Cherry Lake, 2019.

On the Web

With an adult, learn more online with these suggested searches.

Britannica Kids — Plumbing

Kiddle — Plumbing Facts for Kids

Metropolitan Council — Wastewater Treatment for Kids

Glossary

apprenticeship (uh-PREN-tuh-ship) an organized program to learn a skill by working with an expert

auger (AW-guhr) metal spiral bit used to bore holes into various materials

blueprints (BLOO-prints) technical design plans

boilers (BOY-lerz) tanks in which water is heated or hot water stored

crimp (KRIMP) pinch or press together to seal

ductwork (DUHKT-wuhrk) system of pipes and vents used for ventilation or heating

respirator (REH-spuh-ray-tuhr) device worn over the mouth and nose to prevent inhaling dust, smoke, or other toxic substances

solder (SAH-duhr) to join different types of metals together with heat

solvent cement (SAHL-vuhnt sih-MENT) chemical adhesive used to join plastic pipes and parts; also called pipe glue

thread (THRED) cut notches into the pipe so that it can screw into another pipe

wastewater (WAYST-wah-tuhr) water after it is used in processes such as bathing, toilet flushing, laundry, and dishwashing

weld (WELD) to join pieces or parts together permanently using heat or chemicals

Index

activities, 30
apprenticeships, 4, 9, 30

boilermakers, 28
building rules, 12

drainage and sewers, 8, 10, 18
dress and equipment, 20–22, 29

education, 4, 9, 30
energy conservation, 23

fitters, 28
fixtures, 6, 9, 14, 23

green plumbing, 23

hands-on learning, 4, 9, 30
heating, ventilation, and air-conditioning (HVAC) technicians, 29
hygiene, 20–22, 25

installation jobs, 6, 14, 26

jobs and job security, 4, 6, 9, 26–29

licenses and permits, 9, 12, 30

pipe- and steamfitters, 28
pipes, 6–7, 10–13, 16–19, 24, 28

plumbers
job descriptions, 4, 6, 8–19, 26–29
skills, 5, 14–15
tools, 12–13, 16–19, 23, 25, 29
problem-solving, 4–6, 14–15, 19, 25, 28

repair jobs, 6–7, 14–15, 26

safety, 20–25, 28
sewers and drainage, 8, 10, 18
sprinkler systems, 26–27
study and training, 4, 9, 30

toilet paper, 15

wastewater, 8, 10, 18
water conservation, 23